We do it...

A writer or, at least a poet, is always being asked by people who should know better : "Whom do you write for ?" - W.H. Auden

We do it
For that broken child,
Eyes still brimming reflected pain,
We do it
For all the mad ones
And for those who are caged and sane,
We do it
To unravel the nightmares
And the laughter that lullabies pain,
We do it
For all the first times
Words made our pulses beat,
We do it
For desperate drunkards
Trawling for love through the streets,
We do it
For the flotsam
Washed up on the shore,
We do it
For the clumsy
And the over chatty bore,
We do it
To leave a hand print
On the dark cave wall,
We do it
Because we're high-wire dancers
Always about to fall...

The Firekeeper's Tale
I saw for myself.

They got every tribe there is,
Skulls mainly,
Stacked floor to ceiling
And all neatly labelled,
That's what those scientists
Are measuring.

Want to prove
That smarter than dogs,
But dumber than them,
Is what we'll always be.

So for every head,
Man, woman, child,
Even baby

They'll pay handsomely.

Once Upon a Time
There was this Union man
But the Boss found out
And sacked him.

Once Upon a Time
This jobless man
Couldn't pay his rent
So the family got evicted.

Once upon a Time
This homeless man
Couldn't get another job
Because he was blacklisted.

Once upon a Time
This beggar
(Family in the workhouse)
Got sent down for Vagrancy.

Once Upon a Time
This ex-con was dragged off
To the Asylum

While a Boss,
Who was a Landlord
As well as Local Magistrate,
Heartily breakfasted.

In a stone arena
Two men stalk one another :
The Evil Bandit's a Da Vinci Jesus,
All sharp blue eyes and perfect curls

Facing him

Is the Bounty Hunting Vengeful Brother,
A Gentleman reduced to this.

Their boots creak
Like rope
That's neck stretching,
Their spurs chime
Like communion bells.

In the nearby arroyo
Geronimo watches

A small herd of deer

That echoing gunfire
Will suddenly scatter
And the old one
He prayed for

Is soon out of range.

-He told me-

*his Grandmother said,-that when he was
little his Daddy walked him by the old workhouse pointing out burial pits
from the Hunger. He used to lie awake on stormy nights listening to the
wind. He thought it was hungry ghosts wailing.*

*He was a great storyteller. I used to sit by him in the evenings and
he'd puff away on his clay pipe and tell me tales...*

*He'd roses growing just by the front door of the cottage and I re-
member, when I was a little girl, he would never let us cut them. How he'd
say, just open the window a little wider and you'll be able to catch their
scent right enough.*

*In those days the Landlords were always evicting people...there was
one in particular who was universally hated so the Fenians...-*

...he keeps pace with
them his horse easily matching theirs ends up crouching low in the copse
shotgun cocked and loaded then faint at first a distant waterfall riders
and their yoo-halloing hounds shrieking and baying can feel the earth
begin to shudder through the soles of his feet this almighty drumming and
every few seconds an instant of pause as they take the next hedge horse's
hooves rhyming his heartbeat the earth's convulsing in spasms through a
gap in the hedge a fox bursts a bronze comet ears back green eyes glinting
he's away up the meadow right past the old copse hounds shrieking baying
riders follow one's lined up in his sights close enough to see sweat on his
brow gets both barrels jerks back in the saddle blood a fine spray mist at
sunset horse's flanks glistening loses the reins stands tiptoe in the stirrups
crows rise smoke from a burning cottage...

*-he had to leave his
farm and everything behind once they'd got his name. Ended up over here
digging ditches and drinking himself silly every Friday and Saturday night.
And he wouldn't go back, not even after the Treaty...-*

8

A girl stood before him in midstream, alone and still, gazing out to sea.
- A Portrait of the Artist as a Young Man

I've suffered his gaze long enough
Him standing there with his shoes
Round his neck and a bit of old salteaten stick
For a cane well what a grand gallant he makes
Hush now hush now the sea says
And here's a fine gift for you
Hush now hush now maybe he'll speak
And I've suffered his gaze long enough
So bowing my head now maybe he'll speak
Hush now hush now and bending my neck
But see his guilt burn as he turns on his heel
Off away home to his Mammy no doubt
And spinning her lies like a priest.

'Tis Pity...

She wades into the sea
Lace-hemmed and the cold of it
Swells like an artery :
He opens the cut-throat razor
Light trembling on his skin and
The cold of it stings : she's
Knocked back off her heels dragged
In deeper : he follows her
Down now : she senses his pulse :
He follows her down now
Wanting her as she wants him

Mina Harker's Subsequent Biography
She's awake from a nightmare of
Him - *he's been dead twenty years* -
Covered by moonlight, looking
Up through a barred window
At the pale sky and the stars
Fading with no choice but to
Starve for her vote so at dawn
They'll pin her down their *little*
Mouse and as one prays loudly

Force-feed a tube down her throat.

Easter Week
Behind a line of Guinness barrels
Stacked head height across O'Connel street,
Young men in khaki peer through gaps
Look to your front
Caps pulled low, scalps itching
Find your target
Squint away sweat's needle sting
   Take aim
At Poets and slummies
Who pray to Saint Jude

But make every shot count.

There was this boy
Still a child at thirty-five
Who shared a farm
With his old Dad.

The Mammy had
Cleared out years ago
And all she'd left him
Was her eyes.

He endured

Tending beasts,
Rebuilding walls,

Until

One morning
He saw a spade
And his old Dad.

Afterwards
Buried him
In silage.

That night
He went down
To the Pub,
Bought a round
(The first
And last one
Of his life)
Then gave himself up

Just after closing time.

In 1938, Grey Owl, a Native American environmental activist and popular public speaker died suddenly. Within weeks of his death, it was revealed that he was really Archie Belaney, a white man born in Hastings in 1888...

Grey Owl

I remember boots.

Theirs. High buttoned. Dull.

His. Heeled.Tooled leather with shiny toe caps and I grabbed one of them just as he was leaving and they prised my fingers away and scolded me. He turned away then turned back and threw down his hat and said

- Wear that when your head's big enough and remember me.

Then he was gone.

I never saw him again.

My name is Wa-Sha-Quon-Asin, Grey Owl and I come in peace.

They'd say I had his eyes and even when I won the Composition Prize at school, I was still my worthless father's son.

And there was this woman used to watch me sometimes from a distance. I'd be alone, tracking buffalo through the park or hunting bears in our back garden and see her spying through the gaps between the trees. A small dark skinned woman. My mother.

Apparently.

But the two Aunts, my father's sisters, kept her separate. She was The Other and not to be spoken of. So I'd stain my paleface skin with cold tea, stick seagull feathers in my hair, sit on the hillside above the old town dreaming buckskin, beadwork, braided hair and tragedy.

I left first chance I got. Nineteen-o-six. Travelled west. Landed up in Canada. I was supposed to be farming. Ended up at Bear Island, met and married Angele, moved in on what was left of the Anishinabe.

Old Lady cat, my new Grandmother, told me their stories. White Bear taught me how to hunt and track. Go for days on chokecherries and pemmican.

I grew my hair. Peppered my speech with phrases from their language. Walked toe-heel and leaning forward slightly as if the trump line was pressed against my head and I was pulling the weight of a laden sled.

Summers, I guided hunters (white men) and Wintered with the Indians.

They gave me my real name.

.   Nineteen-fourteen, I volunteered.

In France I was stone, dark light, a shattered tree, silent, hours unmoving, waiting for first light and the carelessness it brings. A yawning stretch above the dig-out's lip...a head shot...one less Fritz.

I remember every face

I was Belaney. A. , Honourably Discharged Wounded Great War Veteran, Sniper First Class, bigamist who married a nurse from the Army Hospital then skipped off first chance he got.

Bear Island was more or less deserted. Trees hacked down. Rivers trapped out. Streams choked and dying so one night, drunk on home made wine that had been brewed a full three weeks, burned my discharge papers, smeared the ashes on my white skin and headed back out again.

I killed beaver wherever I could find them. Spent a lot of time alone in my cabin.

And then she came along.

Anahero.

A diner waitress sneered at, groped by drunken white men.

Together we left and every day, she watched me silently. Watched me track and trap and every time I killed, she would turn her face away as my axe fell on some half dead animal, leg gnawed through by my trap and its own desperation until one day

until one day I was about to finish off two beaver kits, deep in the Winter, way out of season and she murmured one word - No!

I never killed again.

Now, from back to backs, from under skies where yellow smoke curls in on itself, they fill every Lecture Hall from Southport to Hastings.

I stand on platform after platform, raise my right hand (I am Grey Owl, Shadow-Who-Flies-By-Night, Wa-Sha-Quon-Asin) and :   One fine morning (I begin) crow noticed a shadow hooked to his foot so he tried to circle it.

Stalking.

        (actions here, arms bent behind my back, elbows hooked out, palms touching)

                But it stalked him.

        (switch roles and in the spotlight, my feet lifting high and slowly like Chaplin)

        So to shake it he'd take off suddenly and row halfway across the sky

        (flapping my arms frantically and them laughing, some applause)

        but wherever he landed, it was waiting for him.

        Finally, at sunset, enraged, he pecked and clawed and caw-caw-cawed at the thing.

        (more laughter, more applause, now they're convinced)

        But then the shadow came to life and simply swallowed him.

        (laughter dies, the faint applause is scattered, echoing)

        I am your shadow

        (they're silent now, listening)

        and when you come to me for sustenance, all I have to offer you is one green leaf.

        I fill every Lecture Hall from Southport to Hastings and they come needing the buckskin, the beadwork that's exquisite, my braided hair, my people's inspiring tragedy.

        I stand on platform after platform, white skin (the mark of Cain) stained with walnut juice, raise my right hand to repeat

        My name is Wa-Sha-Quon-Asin, Grey Owl, and I come in peace...

Blodwen
One man claimed
"I love you"
As triple moons
Waxed and waned
Into her radiant child

Who was stolen away
While papers were signed.

She's been kept
Close confined

As decades crawl by

She draws owls
On the walls

And goes out of her mind.

The Driver's Tale
Dashboard clock says three a.m.
(tonight's arrests begin)
We'd drive through the gates,
(guards snap to attention)
Trees in my headlights
(each one a cornered fugitive)
Road curving to the right,
Salt cracking under our tyres
(if he speaks meet his eyes)
 I take it slowly and sense
(don't move your head)
Him slowly leaning forward
As I park by her grave
(they say she left a note)
He'd get out, pace the edge
(smoky breath feathering)
And once, just once, stop suddenly,
Look round,
Spit
Then cross himself,
Surreptitiously.

Born Dead
Mother's third time
Unlucky but Doctor O'Neill
Wasn't having any so laid on
The healing touch and when
That didn't work was dunked
In hot then cold water repeatedly
Had his chest anointed with whiskey

And so was brought back

A few weeks later
To be laid at the feet
Of Our lady

Queen of Heaven

Mystical Rose

Star of the Sea

But then he grew up

And became me

Whoever that may be.

Fairy Tales (Illustrated)
And there was one
Of a woman bathing,
Back view, half turned
Away, a charcoal *Y*
Of bottom cleavage
Rippling the pool's meniscus
As she, wide-eyed,
Stares at a frog
Lily pad perching,
Who stares, wide-eyed,
Straight back
                while I,
A rising five,
Bones on fire, skin
Like water, sink
Into the page.

And that's
How I was caught
By the reading habit.

In his Perfect Story
A child,
Rejected and despised,
Sits alone in the ashes
Or sets out
With only the stars
For company.

In his perfect story
There will always be
A magic mirror
Never telling the truth
And another
That always lies,
An ancient forest,
Impossible odds,
A once loving heart
Now cold as ice.

In his perfect story
It is always night.

Overheard...
"He was doing Summer Season,
His big come back,
When one night, towards the end of his run,
Some kid starts heckling - upset him terrible -
A few months later : dead,
Heart attack, supposedly
But were that gobby brat did for him..."

Now,
I have this troubling memory
Of Mum, Dad, me -
We're sat Front Circle,
Queen's Theatre, Blackpool -
It's almost the sixties and a red curtain's rising
On his toothy grin, trademark ukulele
When I yell out "That's never him,
's'just some old man !"

He falls into silence.

Coughs.

Whispering.

From the stucco ceiling
Gilded cherubs look down,
Open mouthed,
At a waxwork dummy
That's trying to sing
But he's faded,
Off-key.

So now I know for sure.

It was me.

I killed George Formby.

As the first plate flies...
he's (Dad bellows) running
like hell dives through (Mum
yells) the hedge into long grass

And lies still.

Two ants it ch cra w l across
The back of his hand, a butterfly
(Dad bellows, Mum yells)
Lands takes off again, starlings
Squabble, shadows and leaves
Sculpt a face : closing his eyes
He (Mum and Dad are calling) lies still.

Alma Mater

There are no bells
Ringing
To call
The swooping
Children in.

No desk lids
Slamming,
Squeaky chalk
On unprimed boards,
Chanted prayers
Or off-key hymns.

There are only
Broken windows
And the utter derision

Of crows nesting.

Familiar
In her cottage,
Wattle and daub
Not gingerbread,
The black cat,
Goldeneyes
Swallowing this scene :
A witch,
Half-chewed fragments
Of Greek and Latin
Spilling from her mouth,
Peels willow stalks,
Bruises aromatic leaves.

The scene is familiar
But the cat is not hers.

It's exactly the other way round.

Blackpool : Out of Season
Arcades shuttered,
Prom empty,
Pleasure Beach closed,
Trams in the depot,
The sea
A dirty window.

Over the beach
Sand grains
Advancing retreat advancing
And seagulls
Are wind dancing.

Armchair Fenian
...and turning up the volume
"Who cares what time it is ?"
His heart dances
With its own mythologies
But his head still knows
That behind every Ballad
Is a family squeezed dry
By grief
And another Mother
Ageing visibly...

She lies there sleeping...(for Danielle)

Inside her head
The bewildered ghosts mutter
About disappointment,
The hurting tongue,
A doorway full of seagulls
And three strong memories
Of dancing alone...

What Goes Around...
He became a Priest
"For my Mother's sake..."
This sepia man
Who'll kneel and mouth
Words he reverenced
As a child :
                after Mass,
Scans the Sunday paper for

More Arrests and Allegations

And every keening siren
Will double his heart rate.

"When I am an old woman I shall wear purple
With a red hat..."
- Jenny Joseph

When she was old
She didn't wear purple
Or a red hat
Or spend all her pension
On drink,
She had to work on
Because nobody told her
That having babies
Doesn't let you off
Buying National Insurance Stamps.

Worked on
For a man who was Knighted
For Services to

Tourism I think it was.

Breathed her last
In a Hospice
With whistling Ward Cleaners
As the backing track.

And she never wore purple
Or a red hat.

Another True Romance

1.

"God, listen to her talking,
She sounds like a typical yob,
I'll bet she's the kind of person
Who calls a mouth 'your gob'.

I'll bet she eats 'jam butties'
And goes out drinking every night
And never pops up to the bathroom
But goes off to 'the bog for a shite'.

I'll bet she's never read a real book
Or sat through a decent play,
I'll bet she's a workshy sponger
Who lies in her bed half the day.

I'll bet, yes thanks, I will have another,
That she calls her mother 'Mam'
And that her idea of heaven
Is a wedding ring and a pram.

But God, she has got lovely eyes
And hair like a poet's dream
And when I watch her dancing
It's like gulping an icy stream."

"Would you look at that one staring
Like a daisy drinking the sun,
Mind you, he's got a tight little arse,
Yea, I'd definitely give him one."

2.

"Enjoy this while you can !" she said.
"One fine day you'll wake up,
Look into an empty mirror

And realise your dead."

I nodded sagely
Inwardly scorning her doom
As somewhere nearby
Three old women sniggered

Then went on weaving
At their loom.

3.

"Isn't it terrible
The way things
Slip away from you,
How you blink
And thirty-two
Is forty-nine,
How the week before last
You could drink a pub dry
And now you're content
With a glass of red wine,
Isn't it terrible
How things slip away..."

"You're right there,"
She said and thought
Of her mother
Not quite three years dead.

4.

He clears his throat and begins to read :
"I'd walk the tide-line pocketing shells,
Carefully side-step beached jellyfish,
Race my own shadow as far as the pier,
Get up to the prom for a massive ice-cream :
It was a Summer dream..."

Carefully she waits until
Silence has stretched out enough
And tongue unknotted
Chimes in with : "One year
We stayed in an old caravan
Only our money's lost but Mum
Finds ten bob so Dad has a bet,
His long-shot romps home
At a hundred to one : for the rest
Of that week we picnicked
On the sandy beach,
Played Pontoon for pennies
And Jesus how we laughed..."

"But that's not my memory !" he vainly protests.

"Oh it will be by your next poem," she says.

5.

And sometimes, in the middle
Of some story you've told me before
(Tell it again), sometimes,
When you pause for breath (head
Tilted slightly just to one side),
Sip your drink,
Candlelight catching
Your subtle blue eyes,
It's that moment before
The first time we spoke
And I'm falling in love
        Forever

        Again.

Out of the mouths...
Cold in the dark Bride
Of Christ still unsatisfied
Rising up pushes back the
Coffin lid screws cascade
Rises up pushing back a
Marble lid that tumbles

Silently crashing

She drifts in Our Lady's chapel
There are men talking to women
Who are hatless with children
Running and   not one cowers
When she glares a toddler points

Laughing

And she scatters...

Swing West (i.m. Paul Donnelly - Poet)
There is no-one in this silence
Yet as carefully you pick out
One Selected Poems, the new notebook,
Pages still blank and a pen that's
Fully charged : you saddle up and
Swing West, the rising road before
You, the rising sun at your back.

The light is young.

The day is fresh.

And you come to a clearing
Embraced by white willows,
There's a pool for clean water,
Sweet grass for good grazing,
So you build a slow fire,
Cook bacon and beans.

You know there's no hurry
So sipping cold beer

You'll let the words be.

High-Rise Dwelling
Curtains opened,
About to turn away
And put the kettle on,
He looks down

To garage rooves

Where a hawk
Plucks this headless pigeon,
Then teasing a veil of skin,
Hooks flesh,
Throws back his head
Swallowing,
Looks up

Locks eyes with him.

Yet Another Fractal

After being adored by ants
For the honeydew
Excreted from her back,
She's cocooned inside their nest
Until, silk shell splitting
And resurrected as a butterfly
She totters outside,
Her new wings unfurled,
They curve on the air,
Spinning each breeze
To a twister
That'll wring the trees leafless,
Rip off rooftops,
Stampede waves crag height

While Fundamentalists explain :

Our God is angry ! Our God's in pain !

(Yet again.)